# An INFALLIBLE GUIDE

## TO A Pleasant Wedding

## AND A *Happy Marriage*

History's Best Matrimony Advice

The Enthusiast publishes books and goods for book lovers. Subjects include, vintage how-to, retro-cooking and home economics, holidays and celebrations, games and puzzles, graphic design, classic children's literature, illustrated literature and poetry, humour.

What's Your Passion?

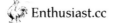 Enthusiast.cc

TheEnthusiast@Enthusiast.cc

EAN
9781595837592

# An

# INFALLIBLE

# GUIDE

## To a

# Pleasant Wedding

## And a

# *Happy Marriage*

# TABLE OF CONTENTS

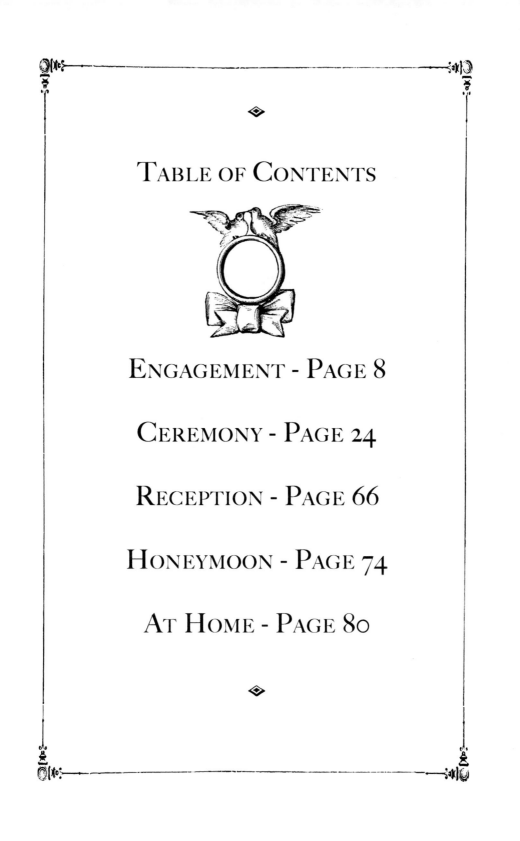

Love does not consist
of gazing at each other,
but in looking together
in the same direction.

*~Antoine de Saint-Exupery*

Engagement

# DIFFERENCES BETWEEN LOVE AND INFATUATION

(READ THIS *BEFORE* DECIDING TO GET MARRIED)

### ~Love~

1. Tends to occur first in late teens and in the twenties.
2. Attachment simultaneously to two or more tends not to be frequent.
3. Most cases last over a long period of time.
4. More slowly develops again after a love affair has ended.
5. Often used to refer to present affair.
6. Object of affection is more likely a suitable person.
7. Parents tend to approve.
8. Broadly involves entire personality.
9. Brings new energy and ambition, and more interests in life.
10. Associated with feelings of self-confidence, trust, and security. Accompanied by kindlier feelings toward other people generally.
11. Joy in many common interests and an ongoing sense of being alive when together precludes boredom.
12. Relationship changes and grows with ongoing association, developing interests, and deepening feelings.

## ~Infatuation~

1. Tends to be more frequent among young adolescents and children under teen age.
2. Simultaneous attachments to two or more tends to be frequent.
3. Tends to last but a short time (only a few weeks in most cases)
4. More quickly reoccurs soon after a given involvement has ended.
5. Is often the term applied to past attachments.
6. Tends to focus more frequently on unsuitable person.
7. Parents more often disapprove.
8. Narrowly focused on a few traits; mostly physical thrill.
9. Less frequently accompanied by ambition and wide interests.
10. Feelings of guilt, insecurity, and frustration are frequent.
11. Tends to be self-centered and restricted.
12. Boredom is frequent when there is no sexual excitement or social amusement.
13. Little change in the relationship with the passing of time.
14. Problems and barriers are often disregarded; idealization may have little regard for reality.

*When You Marry,*
*Evelyn Ruth Millis Duvall, 1945*

## On choosing a husband

When you see a young man of modest, respectful, retiring manners, not given to pride, or vanity, or to flattery, he will make a good husband, for he will be the same to his wife after marriage that he was before it. When you see a young man who is attentive and kind to his sisters or aged mother, who is not ashamed to be seen in the streets with the woman who gave him birth and nursed him, and who will attend to all her wants with filial love, affection, and tenderness, he will cetainly make a very good husband.

*The Wedding Gift: to all who are entering the marriage state,*
*Cotesworth Pinckney, 1849*

# AND, BE SURE TO CHECK YOUR MATE-FINDING MACHINERY

Finally, the young woman knows that it is no longer primarily her parents' job, but hers, to investigate the background and future prospects of the man to whom she is engaged. Presumably she has made certain investigations during the courtship period, or she would not have become engaged. Within the privacy and intimacy of the new relationship the more detailed double checks on their reactions to each other are invaluable. It is incumbent on the pair to carry on this exploration in our crazy-quilt society, because there is no guarantee that our present mate-finding machinery has brought together individuals of similar backgrounds.

*The Book of Weddings: a complete manual of good form in all matters connected with the marriage ceremony,*
*Mrs. Burton Kingsland, 1902*

## ADVICE TO A YOUNG MAN
## ON THE CHOICE OF A WIFE

Many men select their wives by accident. Would it not usually be more appropriate to say that their wives select them? The average man likes to deceive himself when he "goes a-courting" with the idea that he is the pursuing party. He is often pleased with the thought that great difficulties obstruct his efforts in winning the woman of his choice, though in the majority of cases, if, the truth were known, it is the woman and not the man who has made the choice.

*Manhood and Marriage, 1917*

## Here are some of the main purposes of marriage today, both old and new (in case you forget)

1. Marriage provides the most satisfactory answer to the sex problem. Only within marriage is sex both readily available and kept within reasonable bounds.

2. Marriage is essential for society's most important product—persons.

3. Marriage enables the couple to share in spiritual as well as in biological creativity. We hear a lot about how parents raise children. Children also raise parents. To raise

is to lift, to elevate, and to transform with meaning. A baby can elevate a woman into a mother. Children can raise a man to the maturity of responsible fatherhood.

4. Marriage itself is a partnership for the establishment of a family. The uniqueness of the relationship of husband and wife (which is the basis of their property, sex, and other unique relationships) is the common purpose of building a family.

*Before You Marry, Sylvanus Milne Duvall, 1959*

# Try to enjoy the ride

The months and weeks preceding a marriage should be a happy time, if the hearts are in tune — a fond, foolish time between the lovers, when the responsibilities of life are hidden behind rose-colored clouds.

*The Book of Weddings: a complete manual of good form in all matters connected with the marriage ceremony,*
*Mrs. Burton Kingsland, 1902*

# Avoid unseemly nuptials, (despite his impatient ardor)

It is always the bride's privilege to "name the day," as the old phrase has it, which, after consultation with her mother, is submitted to the young man's approval. He, in the ardor of impatient affection, usually pleads for an earlier date, but it is well to place the time at a fitting remoteness, for there is much to be done in the months preceding a wedding. An unseemly rush and hurry is inconsistent with the dignity of the occasion as well as taxing to nerves and temper, and one must take into consideration the delays and disappointments incident to preparations of all kinds. Mutual concessions may, of course, be made, and circumstances sometimes justify very hasty nuptials.

*The Wedding Gift: to all who are entering the marriage state,*
*Cotesworth Pinckney, 1849*

Whatever our souls are made of, his and mine are the same.

~*Emily Brontë*

# First of all, always, always remember, the bride is in charge!

The day of days in a woman's calendar is the one chosen for her wedding — the point of time from which she will reckon all the rest of her life.

The first rule of etiquette concerning weddings is that the bride shall have her own way!

*The Book of Weddings: a complete manual of good form in all matters connected with the marriage ceremony,*
*Mrs. Burton Kingsland, 1902*

# Preparation Lesson
## No. 1
### Make lots of lists

For the invitations four lists are made: the list made by the bride's mother contains the names of relatives and friends in her visiting-list; a similar list is made by the mother of the groom, with the relatives and friends of their family; the bride makes a list of her friends who may not be included in her mother's list; and the groom gives to the bride's mother a list of his friends who may not be on his mother's list, business or professional friends, and college friends, and others whom he wishes to have with him on "the day of days."

*Weddings; modes, manners & customs of weddings*
*by Mrs. John Alexander King, 1927*

# Preparation Lesson
## No. 2
### Yes you are a princess!
### (But on a budget)

Let not the girl who is looking forward to her marriage with the man who has won her heart, and whose character gives assurance that he will keep it, envy the fairytale princesses of whom she reads.  Every girl naturally desires to have a pretty wedding,  and she may do so with the exercise of a little taste and  ingenuity,  without  incurring  expenses that put too severe a strain upon the domestic exchequer.

*Weddings; modes, manners & customs of weddings*
*by Mrs. John Alexander King, 1927*

# Keep Calm
## and Marry On

The advent of a wedding naturally brings much excitement and many cares into the family circle of a prospective bride, and to the bride-elect generally falls the self-appointed task of keeping an eye upon all the arrangements for her entrance into the matrimonial state, selecting her own and her bridesmaids' toilettes, planning the decorations, compiling the invitation list, and keeping herself intimately in touch with affairs in general. It is, of course, perfectly proper for her to do this, if she be so minded; but it is not wise in her so to fatigue herself in preparing for the momentous occasion as to be compelled to enter upon her new life with her nerves shattered and her vitality at its lowest ebb.

*Weddings and Wedding Anniversaries : a book of good form in the conduct of marriage ceremonies, Jean Wilde Clark, 1913*

# DID YOUR CAT JUST SNEEZE?!
## AND OTHER SUPERSTITIONS

In the middle ages it was thought that the union would not be happy if the bridal party in going to church met a monk, priest, hare, dog, cat, lizard, or serpent; while all would go well if a wolf, spider, or toad were encountered.

The sneezing of a cat was anciently considered to be a lucky omen to a lady who was to be married the next day.

In the south of England it is said to be unlucky for a bride to look in the glass after she is completely dressed before she goes to the church; hence a glove or some other article is put on after the last look has been taken at the mirror

*The Wedding Day In All Ages and Countries,*
*Edward J. Wood, 1869*

# Solid suggestions
## for wedding invitations
## and announcements

Use as few abbreviations as possible. *Mr.* and *Mrs.* are, of course, abbreviated, but the names of the month, day of the week, city, state, *Street*, *Avenue*, *Square*, are spelled in full.

The word *and*, not the sign of and (*&*), should be used.

Numbers should be spelled out:  the *fifth of May*; *Five West Ninth Street*

It is not necessary to use any marks of punctuation except the periods after the necessary abbreviations (*Mrs.* for example),  and the apostrophe in *o'clock*

Usually too, a comma is used after the day:
*Tuesday, the First of June*

Instead of using the abbreviation R.S.V.P. to request an answer, it is better to write the request:

*The favor of an answer is requested*
or:
*The favor of a reply is requested to Five West Street*

It is better form to write all names in full rather than to use initials for any of the names:
*Mr. and Mrs. James Russell Brown*

In wedding invitations and announcements the word *honour* is spelled with the U.

*Weddings; modes, manners & customs of weddings,*
*Mrs. John Alexander King, 1927*

# A BRIEF BRIEFING
## ON BRIDESMAIDS

The bride may have as few or as many attendants as she chooses—she may have none, or she may be preceded down the aisle by a procession of ten bridesmaids, a maid of honor (and perhaps a matron of honor also), two flower girls, and, for good measure, have one or two little boys to "attend" her train. But it is the unusual wedding in which there is not at least a maid of honor or a matron of honor. In the average wedding now, there are four or six bridesmaids, besides the chief attendant, who is either a maid of honor or a matron of honor. If the chief attendant is married, she is referred to, conveniently, as the matron of honor. It is the custom for the bride to choose her sister as her maid or matron of honor, or, if she has no sister, her most intimate friend.

When the bride selects her attendants, she usually pays honor to the groom and his family by including among her bridesmaids a sister or cousin of the groom. Sometimes too she invites the groom's sister to be her maid of honor, but usually this place is dedicated to her own sister or the friend whom she has always thought of as attending her on her wedding day. The former dictum that the bridesmaids should be unmarried no longer holds, and now one sees weddings in which as many of the bridesmaids are married as are unmarried. Often all the bridesmaids are married, and it would seem suitable that, if this is the case, the bride should have a matron of honor rather than a maid of honor.

*The Book of Weddings: a complete manual of good form in all matters connected with the marriage ceremony,*
*Mrs. Burton Kingsland, 1902*

# Bridesmaids,
## YOU WILL WEAR THAT DRESS

The bridesmaids must yield unquestioning assent to her preference concerning the color, material, and model of their gowns and all the accessories of their toilettes.

*The Book of Weddings: a complete manual of good form in all matters connected with the marriage ceremony,*
*Mrs. Burton Kingsland, 1902*

## BRIDES, THERE'S A FINE LINE BETWEEN REGAL AND RIDICULOUS

The bride of taste will know the beauty and value of a perfect wedding procession, and she will organize her pageant with that in mind. But she will not allow her procession to become merely a fashion show.

*Weddings; modes, manners & customs of weddings,*
*Mrs. John Alexander King, 1927*

# FLOWER GIRLS

Of the children-attendants, flower girls are most effective and least pretentious. There may be one flower girl to walk in single glory, or two flower girls to walk together, either leading the processional, or, usually, between the maid of honor and the bride. In the recessional, these flower girls still walk together, usually before the bride and groom. The costume of the diminutive flower girl or flower girls should take its cue from the extreme youth of the young lady wearing it. It is not good taste to have the flower girl wear a sophisticated, and therefore inappropriate, frock.

*Weddings; modes, manners & customs of weddings,*
*Mrs. John Alexander King, 1927*

# THE WEDDING GOWN

"There is," said Douglas Jerrold, "something about a wedding gown prettier than any other gown in the world." And this is true whether the bride glitters in wondrous satin or is demure in a simple organdy. Something of the hallowed customs and forms and traditions connected with this ever-old and ever-new ceremony seems to glorify this gown and to imbue it with a mystic loveliness.

*Weddings; modes, manners & customs of weddings,*
*Mrs. John Alexander King, 1927*

## AMERICAN INDEPENDENCE, WHERE WILL IT ALL LEAD?

Now and then one hears of a bride so lacking in sentiment, so indifferent to the traditions cherished by untold generations of brides, as to wear a large round hat with a white wedding gown an ungracious freak of American independence, an injustice to one of our most charming inherited customs. We do not know where such departures may lead.

*The Book of Weddings: a complete manual of good form in all matters connected with the marriage ceremony,*
*Mrs. Burton Kingsland, 1902*

# Choosing
## THE BEST MAN

The best man should not be lightly chosen, nor personal preference alone guide the selection. He should be an executive person, with his wits about him, since those of the bridegroom are apt to desert him at critical moments in his new role, and with whom he feels sufficiently familiar and at ease to say "go, and he goeth; do this, and he doeth it," and so be of real service. In the chapter devoted to the duties of the best man it will be shown how useful that gentleman may be made.

*The Book of Weddings: a complete manual of good form in all matters connected with the marriage ceremony,*
*Mrs. Burton Kingsland, 1902*

## GROOMS, YES YOU ARE AN ACCESSORY, DEAL WITH IT

The bride, by her costume, proclaims the degree of formality of her wedding. And on this great occasion, the bride is queen. The groom ascertains what the bride's wedding costume plans are, and plans his attire accordingly. If the bride feels that her happiness depends on being dressed "like a real bride," in white satin with a long train, a bridal veil, orange blossoms, a shower bouquet, the groom must acquiesce with the best of grace, even if it means that he must buy, beg — or borrow!— the formal clothes that are consistent with and appropriate to this standard of formality.

*Weddings; modes, manners & customs of weddings,*
*Mrs. John Alexander King, 1927*

# REHEARSALS, A NECESSITY, AND AN EXCUSE FOR A PARTY

Rehearsals should be held even for a quiet home wedding, and at a sufficiently early date to insure the presence of all who are to participate.

*A Dictionary of Etiquette : a guide to polite usage for all social functions, W.C. Green., 1904*

# WHEN THE GROOM MAY SEE THE BRIDE, AS IF FOR THE FIRST TIME

The bridegroom must not stay in the same house with the bride the night before the wedding. He must be away and come for her at church, seeing her for the first time when she is brought to him as he awaits her at the altar. This is strict etiquette.

*The Book of Weddings: a complete manual of good form in all matters connected with the marriage ceremony,*
*Mrs. Burton Kingsland, 1902*

# The Bride's Day

The wedding day is the bride's day. In her shimmering bridal gown she is the radiant high-light of the wedding picture. And that she may be "a happy bride" everyone connected with the wedding should contribute a complete and generous spirit of cooperation. On this day of days, the bride's family, the groom, the groom's family, the wedding party, the wedding guests—all pay homage to her.

*Weddings; modes, manners & customs of weddings,*
*Mrs. John Alexander King, 1927*

# Planning the 'Background' for the Bride

After she has planned her own wedding dress, the most important problem that the bride has is the determination of the most beautiful and interesting "background" for that dress, the perfect foil to bring out the perfection of its loveliness. For, in arranging the wedding procession, it will be well to remember that although the social reason for having bridesmaids is the desire of the bride that she shall be attended by her friends, the artistic presentation requires that the attendants, like the lesser jewels of a perfect setting, should enhance the prominence and the beauty of the perfect gem.

*Weddings; modes, manners & customs of weddings,*
*Mrs. John Alexander King, 1927*

# WEDDING DUTIES OF THE BRIDESMAIDS

Besides generous and gracious cooperation with the decree of the bride as to carrying out the details of their costumes, the bridesmaids have not many duties, except to be prompt and helpful at the rehearsal, to be prompt and "pretty" at the wedding, and to receive charmingly and graciously at the wedding reception.

*Weddings; modes, manners & customs of weddings,*
*Mrs. John Alexander King, 1927*

## WEDDING DUTIES OF THE BEST MAN

The best man is the "guide, philosopher, and friend" of the groom on "the" day. His entire day is dedicated to the service of his friend— and the groom usually needs all the attention! He goes, on the morning of the wedding, to the home of the groom, helps him all day in last minute preparations.

*Weddings; modes, manners & customs of weddings,*
*Mrs. John Alexander King, 1927*

# THE BRIDE'S BOUQUET

To fulfill their appealing mission of being the climax of the bridal costume, the flowers in the bride's bouquet seem to be lent an especial glory, a wonder of romance, a delicate mystery that proclaims their sweet importance.

These eloquent ambassadors are too the expression of the time-honored privilege that the groom has of sending the bridal bouquet to his bride.

Whether the bridal bouquet is an exquisite cascade of the flowers traditionally appropriate for the shower bouquet, or an armful of her favorite roses, a spray of exotic white orchids, a delicate bouquet of lilies-of-the-valley, a sheaf of dignified calla lilies, or a gem-like corsage for the simpler wedding, it "seizes a beauty from the skies" and wears it triumphantly.

Since the bridal bouquet must be in harmony with the bridal costume, the groom consults the bride as to her preferences, and interprets them as a devoted cavalier should and would do.

What flowers shall the bride carry? It depends on the style of the wedding gown and the formality of the wedding. If the gown is in the ultra-fashion of the moment, a bouquet should be arranged to be consistent with the details of this fashion. If the gown is of a certain marked period, the flowers should then add the most distinguishing touch to the effect of that period.

But above all, the flowers should be "becoming." That is, they should project the individuality of the wearer. One should feel, when seeing the bridal bouquet, an exquisite sense of completeness.

*Weddings; modes, manners & customs of weddings,*
*Mrs. John Alexander King, 1927*

# The bouquet,
## the final touch

The last touch to the bride's toilet is given when she takes her bouquet, which is always the gift of the bridegroom, and is usually seen for the first time when she is fully dressed. It is always a thing of beauty, of whatever composed — and of sentiment, which goes without saying. A bride rarely forgets to abstract a few of the lovely blossoms, to be tucked somewhere in her dress, to be treasured as a memento of the hour.

*The Book of Weddings: a complete manual of good form in all matters connected with the marriage ceremony,*
*Mrs. Burton Kingsland, 1902*

# Your last moments
## as a single person

It is of the utmost importance that the bride should be fresh and unfatigued—look neither worried nor wearied—and her thoughts free to occupy themselves with the joyous, yet solemn, step that lies before her.

It is etiquette, prescribed by an instinct of womanly dignity, that the bride should be left entirely alone in her own chamber, after she is dressed, for a little while before she leaves it for the last time, that she may "take counsel with God and with her own soul."

*The Book of Weddings: a complete manual of good form in all matters connected with the marriage ceremony,*
*Mrs. Burton Kingsland, 1902*

## YOUR LAST MOMENTS
## WITH MOM AND DAD (SNIFFLE)

Your mother's heart is beating anxiously, but, resolute in her effort to put aside all thought of self in remembering your happiness, she forces smiles to her lips. Your father is doing his best to summon philosophy to his aid and forget that these are his last moments of possession, and that by his own act he must soon give his little girl into the keeping of another—who, at best, is but a human man.

*The Book of Weddings: a complete manual of good form in all*
*matters connected with the marriage ceremony,*
*Mrs. Burton Kingsland, 1902*

# PROCEEDING UP THE AISLE IN AN ORDERLY FASHION

Many styles are adopted for the procession up the aisle. A good order is for the ushers to come first in pairs, then the bridesmaids, maid of honor, and last the bride on her father's arm. At the altar the ushers and bridesmaids open ranks to allow the bride to pass through. This order is usually reversed in the procession down the aisle.

*A Dictionary of Etiquette : a guide to polite usage for all social functions, W.C. Green., 1904*

# THE RING

The ring, in classic times, as now, was placed on the fourth finger of the left hand, because of an erroneous idea that a vein or nerve ran from that finger directly to the heart, and it was thought that the outward sign of matrimony ought to be placed in near connection with that seat of life and the emotions.

*The Book of Weddings: a complete manual of good form in all matters connected with the marriage ceremony, Mrs. Burton Kingsland, 1902*

# Bouquet Tossing

One of the most beautiful of all marriage customs is that of the bride, immediately after the ceremony, flinging her bouquet among her maiden friends. She who catches it is supposed to be the next bride.

*Weddings and Wedding Anniversaries: a book of good form in the conduct of marriage ceremonies, Jean Wilde Clark, 1913*

## Its Ok to Cry

However unlucky or undesirable tears may be on all other occasions, on one's wedding day it is best to shed a few, according to old tradition. They are sure to bring good luck. It is a very excellent thing to wear something borrowed upon the wedding day; it also brings plenty of good luck.

*Weddings and Wedding Anniversaries: a book of good form in the conduct of marriage ceremonies, Jean Wilde Clark, 1913*

Love is a game that two
can play and both win.

~*Eva Gabor*

# THE IDEAL
## GUEST AT A WEDDING

Far too many-people think that for a wedding guest there is no particular obligation other than to see, to hear (and often to eat!) as much as possible. As a return for all the hospitality, the impressive beauty, the courtesy, the friendliness that is extended to them, they often offer only a detached curiosity, an objective interest, a more or less detached participation. They are absorbed in their own reactions, often to the point of being most unpleasantly critical. The kind-minded and therefore kind-mannered guest, on the other hand, realizes a personal responsibility to contribute graciousness and understanding, a friendly participation and appreciation of the infinite pains that have been expended to make a perfect wedding.

*Weddings; modes, manners & customs of weddings,*
*Mrs. John Alexander King, Published 1927*

# TOASTS
## IT'S UP TO YOU

The matter of toasting at the wedding feast is one of individual preference. If toasts are desired, it is the duty of the best man to propose the health of the bride and bridegroom.

The bridegroom responds, usually in a very few words, and the bride bows and smiles in response.

*Weddings and Wedding Anniversaries: a book of good form in the conduct of marriage ceremonies, Jean Wilde Clark, 1913*

# FAMILIES, PLEASE DON'T LOSE IT AT THE RECEPTION

It is a time for mutual tenderness and consideration, best expressed by cheerful courage, smiling faces, and brave efforts to see their own happiness through the eyes of the little lass who has such confident trust that for her no darkness lurks in the unknown future.

*The Book of Weddings: a complete manual of good form in all matters connected with the marriage ceremony,*
*Mrs. Burton Kingsland, 1902*

# THE RECEIVING LINE OR HOW TO AVOID WEDDING CRASHERS

She should stand by her husband's side to receive the best wishes of all present. The guests are not announced, but are introduced by the ushers to the bride if not known to her. The bride should not leave her place to mingle with the guests until all have been introduced to her.

*A Dictionary of Etiquette : a guide to polite usage for all social functions, W.C. Green., 1904*

Our honeymoon will shine our life long: its beams will only fade over your grave or mine.

~ *Charlotte Brontë*

# THE HONEYMOON

# Honeymoon options,
## beyond Niagra falls

Very often, when both the bride and bridegroom are athletic young persons, fond of camping and hunting and outdoor life, the honeymoon is spent in some hunting lodge or camp, and such a one, for those whose tastes run to outdoor life, is ideal indeed. There are, in fact, no hard and fast rules laid down for the choice of the place to spend the honeymoon, since those old days when Niagara was the inevitable choice of every bride. Custom wisely leaves the settling of this to individuals concerned, but a quiet honeymoon in some secluded spot is growing in favor.

*Weddings and Wedding Anniversaries: a book of good form in the conduct of marriage ceremonies, Jean Wilde Clark, 1913*

# LEAVE THE BRIDAL PARTY AT HOME, CONSIDER EUROPE

The honeymoon idea is greatly changed since those days, hardly more than a generation back, when the bridal journey took on the form of a triumphal processional through the country, with members of the bridal party attached to the entourage.

The elaborately planned tour is rather a rare thing in these days, though a European trip is often taken. The wedding trip has become more what good taste demands it should be, one of individual choice, and the destination is a bit of knowledge that belongs only to the persons chiefly interested.

*Weddings and Wedding Anniversaries: a book of good form in the conduct of marriage ceremonies, Jean Wilde Clark, 1913*

# IxNay
## ON THE
## P.D.A.

Young people should not, in the new freedom of betrothal, make themselves conspicuous in public or cheapen their affection by public demonstrations of it. They should not travel about alone, and should observe the same rules of good taste which they regarded before the engagement.

*Weddings and Wedding Anniversaries: a book of good form in the conduct of marriage ceremonies, Jean Wilde Clark, 1913*

# AND AFTER THE HONEYMOON?

THE "honey-moon" is a sweet season, of course. During this period the married couple find in each other their chief delight; they cannot do enough to please each other, but, alas! this happy season is all too short as a rule; a few months generally end it, and bring in its stead neglect and indifference, or worse still, bickering and strife. Will it be so with you? Your conduct will determine.

*The Marriage Guide, 1883*

A happy marriage is a long conversation which always seems too short.

*~Andre Maurois*

# NOTES ON THANK YOU NOTES, WITH AN EXCELLENT EXAMPLE

It should be remembered that gifts are sent from kindness and have been chosen with thoughtful care. Any failure to acknowledge these attentions by a friendly note is an unpardonable lack of politeness.

A card cannot be sent in acknowledgment. A note should be written on paper. Mention should be made of the especial gift that calls forth the thanks, lest it be suspected that the note is a mere duplicate of others.

If a bride is simply to take a short wedding trip it is permissible to acknowledge, after her return, all gifts for which notes had not been sent previously.

There is no precise formula for such a note. Her own good taste and judgment should guide her. Such a note may, however, read as follows:

*Dear Mrs. Hall:*

*"Please accept my most sincere thanks for the beautiful vase you so kindly sent me. I shall appreciate it not only for its worth, but also for the loving thought which prompted it. I trust that we may see you so that we may tell you in person how much pleasure you have given us."*

*Weddings and Wedding Anniversaries: a book of good form in the conduct of marriage ceremonies, Jean Wilde Clark, 1913*

# How to preserve
## the heart you have won

When you shut your door at night, endeavor to shut out at the same moment all discord and contention, and look on your chamber as a retreat from the vexations of the world, a shelter sacred to peace and affection.

If it be possible, let your husband suppose you think him a good husband, and it will be a strong stimulus to his being so. As long as he thinks he possesses the reputation, he will take some pains to do so.

*The Wedding Gift, 1857*

# THE HAPPIEST RELATIONSHIP ON EARTH

Marriage is ideally the happiest relationship in the world, in every way the most satisfying, enchantingly beautiful. It is heaven on earth when it is ideal. It is supreme over all others in the sense that it is the fountain from which all other relationships proceed. There is nothing else like it. In going out of the single life into a true marriage one goes out of earth into heaven.

*The Truth About Marriage, Walter Brown Murray, 1931*

# REGULARLY REFLECT
## UPON YOUR VOWS

The honeymoon is over, and our young couple have exchanged their chrysalis condition for the pleasures and duties of ordinary married life. Let them begin by forming the highest ideal of marriage. Now, and on every anniversary of their wedding-day, they should seriously reflect upon those vows which are too often taken, either in entire ignorance of their meaning and import, or thoughtlessly, as though they were mere incidents of the marriage ceremony.

*How to Be Happy Though Married, E.J. Hardy, 1800*

# SOME OF THE FUN STUFF YOU CAN EXPECT NOW THAT YOU'VE BEEN HITCHED

In addition to the legal requirements, which are for the most part stated in negative terms, we have social requirements more or less enforced which represent the desired levels at which marriage should take place, the social requirements for marriage.

Willingness and ability to carry out the matrimonial obligations of:

1. Sharing a common residence
2. Sexual access
3. Sexual fidelity
4. Conjugal kindness
5. Adult responsibility for homemaking
6. Financial support of dependents

*When You Marry, Evelyn Ruth Millis Duvall, 1945*

# Marriage License.

-State of-    -County of-

The people of the State of _____, to any person legally authorized to solemnize Marriage, **GREETING:** You are hereby authorized to join in the holy bonds of Matrimony, and to celebrate the rites and ceremonies of Marriage, between Mr. _____, and M _____, according to the usual custom and laws of the State of _____, and you are required to return this license to me within thirty days, from the celebration of such Marriage, with a Certificate of the same, appended thereto, and signed by you, under the penalty of One Hundred Dollars.

**Witness** _____, Clerk of our said Court and the Seal thereof, at his office, in _____, in said County, this day of _____, A.D., _____187___.

Seal.

_____
County Clerk.

State of _____, } S.S.   I, _____
_____ County.   a _____, hereby certify that on the _____ day of _____, 187___, I joined in Marriage, Mr. _____, and M _____, agreeable to the authority given in the above License, and the customs and laws of this State.

Given under my hand and seal, this _____ day of _____, A.D., 187___.

_____
SEAL.

## MARITAL RELATIONS
## (HINT: CONTINUE THE COURTSHIP)

The husband should first of all make up his mind that the wife is to be the controlling factor in all sexual relations. If during marriage he continues the conditions of courtship, and the lovemaking associated therewith, her instincts will always indicate the time when the marital relation may be wisely entered into. He will soon understand her attitude from her responses to his caresses.

*Manhood and Marriage, by Bernarr Macfadden, 1916*

## ACHIEVING TRUE UNITY

Happiness in marriage is dependent not alone on perfecting the physical sex act to the point of mutual fulfillment. As studies and clinical evidence have richly indicated, it lies more within the personality adjustment of each member of the couple and in their larger relationships as two whole persons than in any physical tricks or techniques. True married living revolves around such interchange as is found in planning for the children, spending the family money, making plans for vacations and holidays, rejoicing over personal advances, and comforting one another in times of illness or disappointment. It is these day-by-day experiences in common that set the stage for the fullness of sexual response which, for most couples, symbolizes their unity, and is far more satisfying than the purely physical release involved.

*When You Marry, Evelyn Ruth Millis Duvall, 1945*

## BE COURTEOUS

Treat your wife with the courtesy that you would exact for her from other men. Among the lesser means for keeping the flame of love alight are the outward forms of courteous observance, which erect barriers against a too frank expression of opposing or unwelcome sentiments, compelling gentle tones
and self-controlled bearing.

*The Book of Weddings: a complete manual of good form in all matters connected with the marriage ceremony,*
*Mrs. Burton Kingsland, 1902*

## AND MAKE AN EFFORT

Many women too often seem to think, that the marriage ceremony having been completed, there is no further need for that becoming adherence to the proprieties of dress, which have been in some degree a cause of attraction. They fancy that they are then only married women, and by their negligence in their dress, openly confess that the art of love has been but an artifice, and their husbands the dupes. A woman who is wise should commune with herself deeply on this head. The effort which was an act of inclination before her marriage, she should consider as a point of duty afterwards.

*The Wedding Gift, 1857*

## USE HONEYED WORDS
## AND DAINTY COMPLIMENTS

Do not give up the habit of expressing your affection. As time goes on the characteristic shyness of the Anglo-Saxon will impose a reserve that becomes habitual and hard to break. You feed her now with the sugar-plums of honeyed words and dainty compliments. See that you do not let her hunger later for the daily bread of assurance that she is fondly loved if you would see her at her best.

Love cannot be taken for granted, and living on the memory of what has been said is like trying to warm one's self with last year's sunshine. Remember, too, that praise is the best incentive and inspiration to continued excellence.

*The Book of Weddings: a complete manual of good form in all matters connected with the marriage ceremony,*
*Mrs. Burton Kingsland, 1902*

# 8 WAYS OVERCOME
## THE HUM DRUM

Even a life that is free from hardships and unpleasantness may become dull and tedious through its day-after-day sameness.

This danger can be avoided by:

1. Taking short trips
2. Going on week-end vacations
3. Attending movies or the legitimate theater
4. Attending popular lectures
5. Dining out now and then
6. Visiting the homes of friends
7. Entertaining friends at home
8. Arranging record or radio concerts at home

These are but a few of the possible ways of breaking the monotony of domestic life.

*Marriage Guidance; a study of the problems of the married and of those contemplating marriage, Edwin F Healy, 1958*

## SIMPLY BE POLITE, AND GIVE EACH OTHER SOME SPACE

The primary cause of friction between married persons is selfishness on the part of one or both. You must be careful not to become absorbed in your own interests only. Do not insist on your way of doing things, on your preferences in various matters.

It is well for you to give each other a reasonable amount of independence and liberty in the matter of companionship. Everyone wishes to be accorded some solitude, to have some period of time when he can be alone with his thoughts, and also to enjoy some association with others.

A husband should be permitted to be away from home one or two nights a week. A wife should feel free to spend one day a week with friends.

In their dealings with each other husband and wife should not neglect the ordinary courtesies. Even when the two are dining together alone it is a mistake to disregard the conventional manners at table. The use of "please" and "thank you" must not be reserved for strangers. Husband and wife should see that they are at least as courteous to each other as they are toward friends and acquaintances.

*Marriage Guidance; a study of the problems of the married and of those contemplating marriage,*
*Edwin F Healy, 1958*

# SOLID ADVICE ON
## CONSOLATION AND CONGENIALITY

Even though the subject matter appears to you to be very trifling or uninteresting, listen attentively to your wife's conversation. She should be able to find in you a sympathetic listener. She has a right to look to you for consolation in her trials and for advice in managing the affairs of the home. Do not let the reading of newspapers or magazines prevent you from engaging in a reasonable amount of conversation with your wife. Try always to look cheerful. Smile often. A frowning brow is a hindrance to congeniality.

*Marriage Guidance; a study of the problems*
*of the married and of those contemplating marriage,*
*Edwin F Healy, 1958*

# AND AVOID BEING UNCOUTH OR INCONSIDERATE

Husbands must remember to be gentle and considerate in all their dealings with their wives. Rough speech, coarse actions, unmannerly conduct, grate on a woman more than most men realize. A wife desires her husband to be a gentleman on all occasions. Anything in him that is uncouth or offensive to good taste disappoints and hurts her.

*Marriage Guidance; a study of the problems of the married and of those contemplating marriage, Edwin F Healy, 1958*

## LISTEN TO EACH OTHER'S COMPLAINTS (OR AT LEAST PRETEND TO)

An important point for a wife to remember is that she must actively cultivate her husband's love. She should often manifest signs of her affection for him, and she should endeavor to keep his love for her alive by trying always to be genuinely feminine. By exercising great care with regard to her personal appearance, even when she is alone with him, she will minimize the risk of losing her attractiveness in his eyes. A little effort on her part will help her to discover new ways of pleasing him. She should show originality in the preparation of meals. She should make the home an attractive haven to which he will be happy to come.

There should be in the home an atmosphere of peace and simple comfort. Few things interfere with domestic harmony more than nagging on the part of the wife.

She must avoid criticizing her husband regarding faults which he cannot or will not correct, for such criticism is fruitless and will grate on his nerves. His failure in business undertakings, the faults and foibles of his relatives, the mistakes of his past life—these should not be formed into an unforgettable indictment that haunts his hours at home.

*Marriage Guidance; a study of the problems of the married and of those contemplating marriage, Edwin F Healy, 1958*

# AND FINALLY, MORE OCCASIONS FOR MERRY-MAKING

It is a charming idea to celebrate the different anniversaries by some simple form of entertainment. Include, if possible, in your invitations all the guests who were with you on your wedding day, although a cozy little dinner, to which are bidden the bridesmaids, ushers and intimate friends, will be the most effective celebration. Fanciful divisions of the years into shorter epochs than mark the silver, golden or diamond weddings are frequently accepted as occasions for merry-making. Of these the wooden, tin, and crystal weddings are those most commonly observed. Other anniversaries, also described in the following pages, are occasions not neglected by the lovers of merriment.

Wedding Anniversaries have been recognized by the following titles for many years and are variously celebrated:

* One year, Cotton Wedding
* Two years, Paper Wedding
* Three years, Leather Wedding
* Five years, Wooden Wedding
* Seven years, Woolen Wedding
* Ten years, Tin Wedding
* Twelve years, Silk or Linen Wedding
* Fifteen years, Crystal Wedding
* Twenty years, China Wedding
* Twenty-five years, Silver Wedding
* Thirty years, Pearl Wedding
* Thirty-five years, Lace Wedding
* Forty years, Ruby Wedding
* Fifty years, Golden Wedding
* Seventy-five years, Diamond Wedding

*Weddings and Wedding Anniversaries: a book of good form in the conduct of marriage ceremonies, Jean Wilde Clark, 1913*

CPSIA information can be obtained at www.ICGtesting.com
Printed in the USA
LVOW11s1847061114

412380LV00003B/201/P